THE TIPI (tepee) was not a simple tent—it was a sophisticated dwelling designed and built with enormous skill to meet the demands of life on the Great Plains. With a straightforward text and clear line drawings, author Charlotte Yue and architect/artist David Yue describe the elements of the tipi, its structure and furnishings. This leads naturally into a broader look at Native American life: the constant search for food and the battle against a harsh environment; the legends, social life, and the abiding spirituality. There were tipis for chiefs, tipis for religion, tipis for joyous gatherings and for grief as well.

In addition, *The Tipi* tells of the Indians' total dependence on the buffalo for their way of life. When white hunters destroyed the vast herds that had ruled the plains, Native American life passed like a vision. That vision, in all its complexity and color, comes alive in the drawings and prose of *The Tipi*.

# THE TIPI

## A Center of Native American Life

## by David and Charlotte Yue

ALFRED A. KNOPF
NEW YORK

*To Frances and Timothy*

*This is a Borzoi Book Published by Alfred A. Knopf, Inc.*

Copyright © 1984 by David and Charlotte Yue
All rights reserved under International
and Pan-American Copyright Conventions.
Published in the United States by
Alfred A. Knopf, Inc., New York,
and simultaneously in Canada by
Random House of Canada Limited, Toronto.
Distributed by Random House, Inc., New York.
Book design by Mimi Harrison
Manufactured in the United States of America
2 4 6 8 0 9 7 5 3 1

Library of Congress Cataloging in Publication Data
Yue, David.
The Tipi: A Center of native American life
Summary: Discusses the Great Plains Indians,
the land on which they lived, and the tipis they built.
1. Indians of North America—Dwellings—Juvenile literature.
2. Indians of North America—Great Plains—Juvenile literature.
[1. Indians of North America—Dwellings.   2. Dwellings.
3. Indians of North America—Great Plains]
I. Yue, Charlotte.   II. Title.
E98.D9Y83 1984   728   83-19529
ISBN 0-394-86177-9      ISBN 0-394-96177-3 (lib. bdg.)

*Jacket painting from* Cow Landscape *by J. H. Sharp*
*Private Collection Courtesy of Kennedy Galleries, Inc., N.Y.*

# CONTENTS

# THE TIPI

# THE·PEOPLE
# AND
# THE·LAND

CHAPTER ONE

## *The People Who Lived in Tipis*

An encampment of tipis on the Great Plains must have been an awesome sight—a large circle of cone-shaped tents standing majestically against the flat landscape.

Tipis were the homes of the Blackfoot, Cheyenne, Crow, Dakota or Sioux, and other people known as the Great Plains Indians. Nobody knows when or how the tipi developed. In 1541, the Spanish explorer Coronado described tipis he saw when he journeyed into the Great Plains, but tipis may have been in use long before then.

Some anthropologists think that the ancestors of the

3

Great Plains Indians once lived in the wooded areas on the outskirts of the plains, planting some crops and traveling into the plains only on seasonal hunting expeditions. They may have lived in wood or bark shelters and used small tipis as temporary shelters when they were hunting.

Wherever they went, they traveled on foot. All their belongings were carried with them—hauled by large, strong dogs and carried in packs on their backs. Indians refer to these olden times as the Dog Days.

The Indians gradually expanded their hunting range and ventured deeper into the plains. Eventually the Great Plains became their only home, hunting provided their main food supply, and tipis became their only dwellings.

In the Dog Days there were no horses in this country. Horses were first brought to North America in 1541 by Spanish settlers and explorers. When Indians first saw horses they called them names that meant "big dog" or "mysterious dog" or "elk dog" because they were about the size of elk. By around 1650, Indians were learning to ride and were acquiring horses from Spanish settlers in the Southwest. The use of horses spread northward from tribe to tribe.

The lives of the Indians changed dramatically as they became skilled horsemen. Hunting on horseback was much easier and more successful, so food became more plentiful. Now the people could travel farther, and tribes migrated throughout the Great Plains. Tipis were adopted by more tribes. With horses available to haul them, the tipis became larger. People began to have more furnishings and belongings—not just the absolute necessities. By 1820 the Indians were the lords of the plains.

At that time, before European settlers started building towns there, the Great Plains was a nearly featureless, flat grassland. It did not have many trees or mountains, and it seemed to stretch endlessly. Before the land was used for farms, the wealth of the Great Plains was in the vast herds of buffalo. Because the Great Plains Indians depended on the buffalo for food, clothing, and shelter, they did not live in one place, but moved to follow the herds.

Indians lived in family groups or hunting groups. One community or band rarely had more than a hundred people of all ages. A few bands might camp together, and several bands might consider themselves part of the same tribe. The tribe would gather for certain ceremonies or for a tribal council. But each band was independent, with its own head man or chief. At any time a band might leave and camp apart or join another band or group of bands. When a band became too large, some of the people would form a new band with a new leader.

Each band hunted within a different part of the tribal territory, so that everyone could get a fair share of the available game and resources. These divisions were not intended to denote ownership of the land by any one band or tribe. Indians believed that no man could own land, rivers, or game. Each person took what he needed, but no one tried to accumulate more than he could use. People who were sick or helpless or too old to provide for themselves were taken care of by the tribe. Wealth was measured more by what a person gave to others than by what he owned.

## What It Was Like to Be an Indian Child on the Great Plains

All children had a place in the tribe. They were expected to help and to learn the skills they would need in later life. Children were very important and well loved. Grandparents spent a lot of time teaching their grandchildren and caring for them while the parents were busy.

Babies were put in a cradle-board or papoose-board. A rawhide basket, a rolled-up hide with the fur left on for warmth, or a buckskin case that laced up the front was attached to a board or to stiffened pieces of rawhide. The cradle-board kept the baby out of harm's way, and it could be carried easily on the mother's back. Many were elaborately decorated, with rattles and trinkets attached to keep the baby amused.

Children listened to stories, visited friends, played with toys, and took part in competitions and games. They played many kinds of ball games, target-practice games, and games of dice and counting sticks. There were team games and games that could be played by a few friends. Indian children also ran races, including horse races.

They all learned to ride horses, beginning their lessons as soon as they could sit astride a pony and hold the reins.

Girls played with dolls dressed in deerskin. They sometimes carried dolls on their backs in toy cradleboards. When girls were old enough, they helped carry water. As they grew older, they began to gather fuel and wild roots and berries. When they were about twelve years old, girls were taught to cook, sew, prepare hides, and make and set up tipis. Girls generally were married by sixteen.

Boys were taught mostly by their grandfathers. They

learned to ride as well as to make and use bows and arrows. By four or five, a boy was expected to manage his own pony. By six he had a bow and was shooting with blunt arrows. The grandfather taught him tribal history and legends, traditions and religion. Boys learned the importance of quietness and caution when stalking game. They learned to observe the habits of animals—where they could be found, and how they behaved. They were taught to use the wind, the plant life, and the features of the landscape to the best advantage. Boys learned to understand the prairie.

## What the Great Plains Was Like in Indian Days

Indians knew the land they lived on, and their homes were well adapted to the conditions of that land. Their tipis kept them warm in the winters, cool in the summers, and were light enough to be moved from place to place. After a hard day of traveling, two women could set up a tipi in about fifteen minutes. The tipi offered safety and comfort as well as beauty and luxury.

Many modern buildings are uncomfortable and cheerless because we often underestimate the power of nature and overestimate our own ability to use technology to overcome the forces of nature.

A tipi was designed to be used on the Great Plains. To understand how the tipi was structured to provide protection from high winds, driving rains, hail, snow, and burning sun, it is important to understand the land.

The Great Plains is a huge area in North America between the Missouri River Valley and the Rocky Mountains. It reaches up into Canada and stretches down to Texas.

When the Indians were the lords of the plains, it was open grassland. Mile after mile of rolling hills with swaying, rippling grasses made the land look like a sea of grass. The Great Plains was also called the land of the great sky since there was an uninterrupted view of endless blue. Occasional ranges of hills stood out from the vast stretches of level ground.

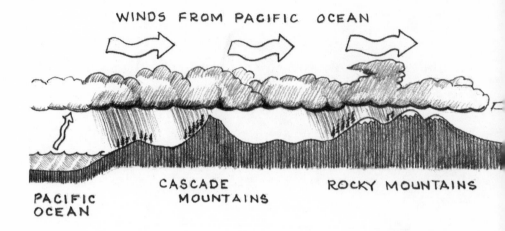

WINDS FROM PACIFIC OCEAN

PACIFIC
OCEAN

CASCADE
MOUNTAINS

ROCKY MOUNTAINS

It was a land of intense colors. Sunsets were spectacular displays. As different flowering plants bloomed in season, the tawny grasses were brightened with changing patterns of purple, blue, gold, pink, red, and silver. In winter the Great Plains was somber and desolate, an enormous area of gray and white.

The Great Plains could be a place of startling beauty; but because of its geography, it could also be a very harsh place to live. Moist winds coming from the Pacific Ocean lost most of their moisture as they were cooled in the western mountain chains. By the time the winds crossed the Rockies, there was little moisture left. It was not until much farther east that moist winds coming from the Gulf of Mexico brought any substantial rain to the land. The vast area in between was warm, windy, and dry. East of the Rockies, winds could blow unstopped for great distances across the flat landscape. Grasses thrived in the dry soil and were unharmed by the winds.

WINDS FROM
GULF OF MEXICO

...IN SHADOW

...REAT PLAINS

APPALACHIAN
MOUNTAINS

ATLANTIC
OCEAN

But there was not enough water in the soil to support trees, and many young plants were damaged by the high winds.

The Great Plains was a land of extremes in climate—scorching summers and bone-chilling winters. There were long dry spells and sudden flash floods, fierce summer hailstorms and brutal winter blizzards.

Changes were often quite sudden. There might be a violent, blinding downpour, and a moment later the sun would be shining brightly. Snowstorms were severe. But a chinook (pronounced *shi*-NOOK), a flow of warm, dry air from the mountains, could raise temperatures enough to melt a foot of snow overnight. Seemingly out of nowhere, lightning could start a wildfire raging—Red Buffalo, as it was called by the Indians—leaving a trail of burned, blackened earth.

Nevertheless, for the many plants, animals, birds, and insects that adapted to the environment, the Great

Plains provided a bountiful home. In addition to the abundant grasses, flowering herbs and woody shrubs thrived on the Great Plains. Hordes of burrowing animals—prairie dogs, ground hogs, and gophers—plowed the soil. The air was vibrant with flapping wings and the chirps and calls of insects and birds—golden eagles, red-tailed hawks, grouse, and prairie chickens. The vast grassland fed huge herds of grazing animals—elk, deer, and bison—patrolled by wolves, coyotes, and grizzly bears.

The largest animal of the Great Plains was the magnificent American bison or buffalo. These animals were so plentiful that at times the land was covered by them as far as the eye could see. Single herds were estimated

at several million. Travelers reported crossing a procession of bison that was a hundred miles wide and never seemed to end. Buffalo was the area's major natural resource. The Indians not only ate buffalo, but used it to make clothing as well as tools and utensils. They also cooked their food and heated their homes with fuel from the buffalo, lived in a tipi made from its hide, and worshiped the animal that gave its flesh to keep their people alive.

The Indians who lived on the Great Plains knew the different sounds and tastes of the wind. They understood the whistle, the rumble, the roar of the wind, the sweet-tasting breezes blowing from flower fields. They knew where to find the running streams and springs. They had knowledge of healing herbs, of when and where to gather berries and roots. They understood the movements and cries of the plains animals. The Indians lived as part of a community, sharing the land with its other inhabitants.

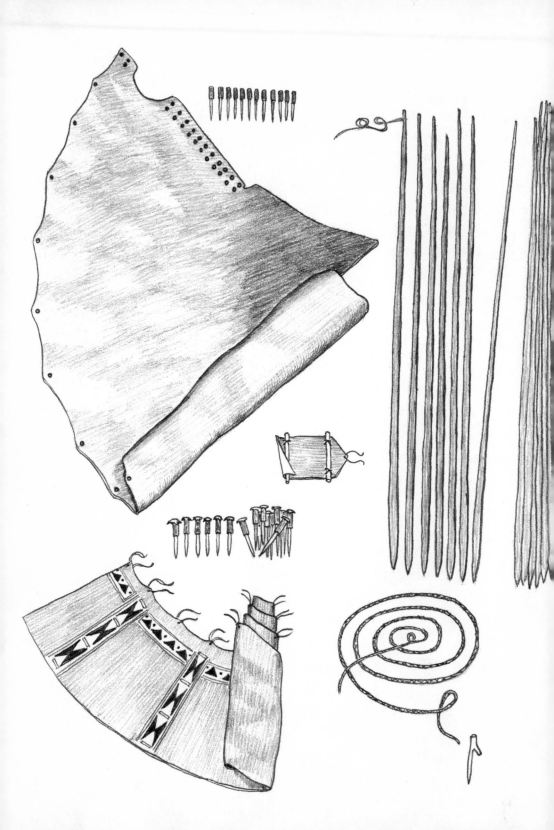

# STRUCTURE
# OF·THE
# TIPI

CHAPTER TWO

*The Parts of the Tipi, How They
Worked, How They Were Arranged,
How They Were Adapted to Meet
the Conditions of the Great Plains*

The name *tipi* means "used to dwell in." It comes from
two Dakota words—*ti* meaning, "to dwell," and *pi*
which means, "used for." Although the structure of the
tipi seems simple, it was carefully engineered to create
a practical, livable home: well lighted, well ventilated,
cozy in winter, sturdy in high winds, and dry in heavy
rains.

The tipi was constructed of a frame of wood poles
arranged in a cone shape. This framework was enclosed

15

by a cover of buffalo hides. A cone shape can withstand very strong winds. It is very difficult to blow over a cone because there is no place for the wind to catch hold. Since there are no pockets or folds to catch water, it also sheds rain well.

A small open fire in the center of the tipi provided sufficient heat and light as well as a stove for indoor cooking. Smoke was let out through a vent, an opening at the top of the tipi.

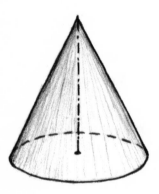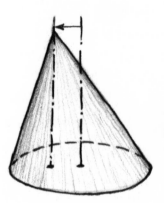

If the tipi were a true cone, the vent would have to be in the center of the top at the crossing of the poles. The opening would need to be large, and it could never be completely closed in wet weather. The Indians solved the problem by tilting the cone. This placed the smoke

16

vent toward the front of the tipi along the longer, sloping side. The poles crossed at the top of the smoke hole instead of in the middle.

Tilting the cone made the back of the tipi shorter and steeper. Since the door of the tipi usually faced east, the short, steep side formed a strong brace against the winds, which generally came from the west in the Great Plains. And the morning sun shining into the tipi gave welcome warmth and light.

Two flaps extended from the cover at the smoke hole like two ears. Two poles were attached to the flaps outside the tipi. By moving the poles to adjust these flaps, the Indians could keep wind and rain out of the smoke hole. The flaps could be crossed to close the smoke hole completely.

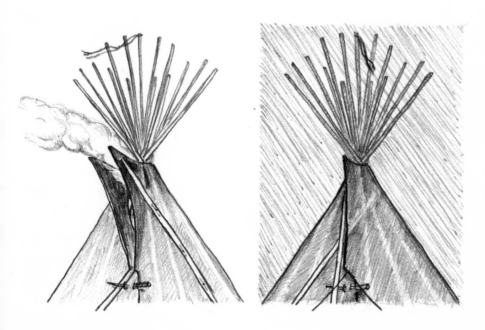

SIDE ELEVATION

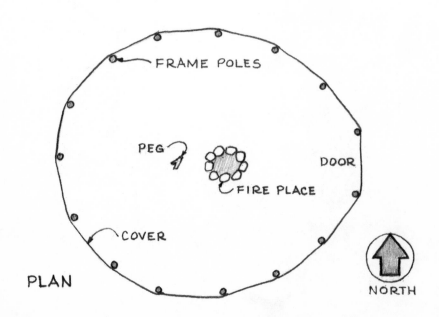

FRAME POLES

PEG

FIRE PLACE

DOOR

COVER

PLAN

NORTH

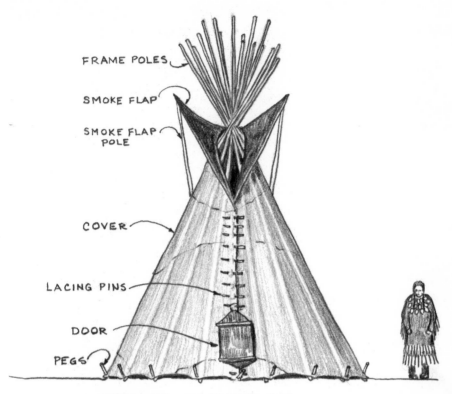

FRAME POLES

SMOKE FLAP

SMOKE FLAP POLE

COVER

LACING PINS

DOOR

PEGS

FRONT ELEVATION

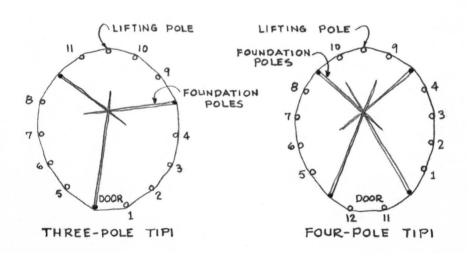

LIFTING POLE

11   10

9

8

FOUNDATION POLES

7

4

6

3

5

2

DOOR

1

THREE-POLE TIPI

LIFTING POLE

FOUNDATION POLES

10   9

8

4

7

3

6

2

5

1

DOOR

12   11

FOUR-POLE TIPI

The number of poles used would vary, depending on the size of the tipi and how far apart the poles were placed. An average tipi needed fifteen poles for the frame and two more for the smoke flaps.

If you tried to tie fifteen sticks together and arrange them to stand evenly spaced without falling over, you would soon realize that constructing this framework took a great deal of skill. The fact that poles used for an average tipi were over twenty feet long further complicated the task.

The tipi, like any good structure, had a foundation which gave the underlying support for the whole tipi. Three or four of the poles were tied together and set up first. This tripod or quadripod was the foundation. All the additional frame poles were then arranged between the foundation poles. These strengthened the structure and gave it its circular form.

Whether a three-pole or four-pole foundation was used depended on the tribe and its traditions. Some tribes were three-pole people, and some were four-pole people. The size of the tipi did not matter. All tipis were structured on a three- or four-pole foundation.

The Indians also developed a definite order for arranging the additional poles. Haphazardly placed poles might clog the vent and make the tipi smoky inside. It might be impossible to fit the cover smoothly over a disorderly frame or to close the smoke hole completely. Most of the frame poles rested in the V shape formed at

the top, front of the foundation poles, away from the cover at the back. The poles were neatly positioned in a fixed pattern in order to keep the place where they crossed as trim as possible. A tight-fitting cover made for a snug lodge.

21

Since the tipi was a tilted cone, the inside floor plan was egg-shaped. If it were a true cone, the floor would be a circle. The floor was longer from back to front than it was from side to side. The curve at the back of the tipi was slightly flattened, giving a little more floor space at the rear of the lodge. The tilted cone also provided more head room at the back of the lodge where there was more activity.

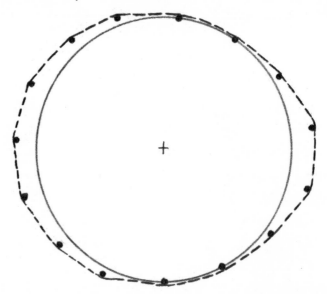

The tipi would be higher at the point than most rooms, about fourteen feet from the ground. But since the walls sloped, it would feel like an attic inside. There was plenty of room to walk around in the middle. But in other parts it was necessary to bend or crawl. The lowest area was used for storage, sitting and sleeping.

Tipis were as beautiful as they were practical. If you

walked around a tipi and looked at its form, the tilted cone would appear different from every direction. Tipis were elegant, graceful structures, and the camp circle must have been a grand and stately community.

## Tipi Construction and the Role of Women

Tipis were made—and usually owned—by women. The women made the furnishings and decided how they were to be arranged inside. They selected the camp site, put up the tipis, and took them down. Except during certain ceremonies and formal occasions, women had authority in the home. In some tribes, a woman divorced her husband by putting his belongings outside her tipi.

Men were hunters and warriors. They never helped or took any part in work around the lodge. Sometimes men needed more than one wife to do all the work.

There were guilds of women similar to warrior societies of men. A woman's reputation as a housekeeper was important. There was rivalry among women and boasting about domestic accomplishments, just as there was among men about skills as a hunter or fighter. A well-made tipi, properly erected, was a matter of great pride to a woman. The materials they used for their tipis were carefully selected and prepared.

## *Lodge Poles*

Lodge poles were difficult to obtain on the treeless prairie. Indians took very good care of the ones they managed to get, but the poles had to be dragged from camp to camp and usually needed to be replaced every year or two. Indians made long journeys to the foothills of the mountains at the edge of the plains to get new poles. Cheyenne people frequently traveled from Oklahoma to Montana for their lodge poles. Sometimes poles were purchased, and they were valued quite highly. One horse could buy about five poles.

The number and length of the poles that could be obtained determined the size of the tipi. The smallest lodges had about twelve poles, the largest over thirty. Lodge poles had to be longer for larger tipis.

Women gathered poles in the early spring as soon as it was possible to travel. They wanted poles that were tall, straight, slender, and would not rot or split. Most often they used pine trees. Poles from cedar trees were light and strong. And poles from fir trees, when available, were even lighter.

Trees were carefully selected. The women peeled off the bark and made them as straight and smooth as pos-

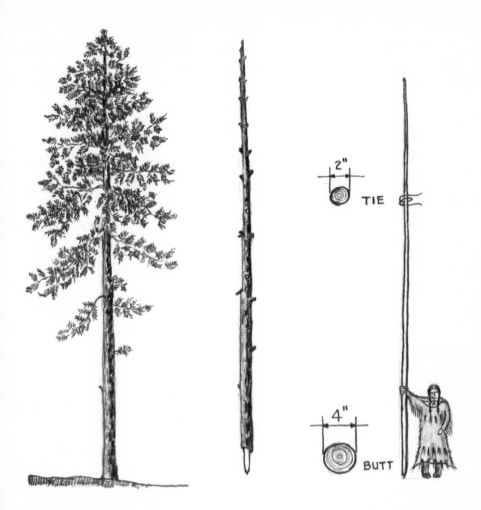

sible. Lodge poles needed to be 21 to 25 feet long, 3 to 4 inches thick at the bottom or butt, tapering to about 2 inches where the poles were crossed and tied. Smoke-flap poles were somewhat smaller—about 2 inches thick at the butt. The butts were carved to a point, and the pointed bottoms kept the poles from slipping on the ground.

After the poles were prepared, they were seasoned for at least three weeks. This was done by setting up the frame just as it would be in a finished lodge and letting the poles stand and dry in the sun and air.

The cover had to stretch tightly around the frame. Well-made poles would stay rigid and not bend or curve. And they needed to be perfectly smooth so that rain would run straight down them to the ground instead of dripping into the tipi. Crooked or poorly trimmed poles gave a woman a bad reputation as a housekeeper.

## The Tipi Cover

When laid out flat on the ground, a tipi cover looked like a semicircular, sleeveless cape with long lapels near the middle of the straight side. In fact, it functioned like a cape, too. It was wrapped completely around the frame and fastened in the front. The lapels could be adjusted to shield the smoke hole in wind or rain.

An average-size lodge required twelve or fourteen buffalo hides. Hides from older buffalo cows killed in the early summer were best for making tipi covers. These cows had shed their winter fur. Their hides were thinner, easier to tan, and lighter to transport from camp to camp.

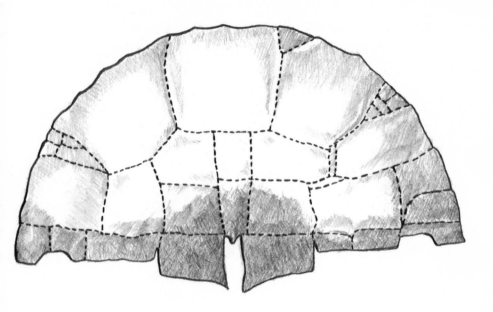

Tanning hides was a long and tedious process. Women had to prepare the hide, apply the tanning mixture, and work the skin to make it soft and easy to bend and shape. First the hide was fleshed—all the flesh, fat, and blood was scraped off it. Using scrapers made from buffalo bones, the women scraped the hide until it was the right thickness all over. It was then left in the sun for several days to bleach and cure. The most commonly used tanning mixture was made of buffalo brains, liver grease, basswood bark, soapweed, and water. Women applied this mixture to both sides and rubbed it in with their hands or with a stone. Then the hide was left outside again so that the heat from the sun would help the tanning mixture penetrate the hide evenly. The hide then had to be stretched and rubbed and dried to soften the texture and make it supple. The process would be repeated until the hide was as soft and pliable as needed.

A tipi cover did not last more than a year or two. Old lodge covers were not discarded. They were used to make moccasins and other clothing.

Making a new cover was a community project somewhat like a quilting bee. A woman making a new cover invited other women to a feast. By accepting her invitation, the others showed they were willing to help. All women learned to make clothing, bags, and other small articles, but only a few women became expert at designing and cutting tipi covers. One woman who was skilled at making covers would be invited to supervise the project. Some women would prepare the thread, which was made from fibers of buffalo tendon called sinew. Other women would do the cutting, while still others did the sewing. Small, delicate buffalo bones were used for sewing needles. The woman in charge looked over the hides and told the others how to arrange them, where to cut, and how to patch the hides together.

The new cover was pure white. When it was completed, it was put on the frame with the smoke vent completely closed and a fire burning inside the tipi. Smoking the skin made the cover waterproof. A cover that had been smoked would always retain its softness even when soaked by rain. After smoking, the tipi was a cream color.

The tipi cover was translucent, which meant that some light would shine through the skin. A tipi was never dark or gloomy inside. At night the fireplace would light up the inside of the tipi. From the outside, a tipi seen at night would glow like a lantern, radiating a soft, flickering light.

When trade with settlers made canvas available to the Indians, that material was used instead of buffalo hides for making lodge covers. Canvas covers were easier to make. They did not require the long tanning process or the difficult cutting and patching that was necessary with hides. Canvas tipis could be larger, since the material was lighter, but the basic design of the cover remained the same.

# TIPI·CAMPING ON·THE GREAT·PLAINS

## CHAPTER THREE

### *Camp Sites*

When choosing a good place to pitch camp, the Indians had to consider many factors. Availability of fresh water, food, fuel, and grass as well as the safety and convenience of the site were all very important.

Trees were scarce on the prairie, and tipis were designed to be comfortable without any shade. Even if a camp site was near a clump of trees, the tipi would not be set up directly under them. Trees are dangerous when there is lightning or violent winds. And a tipi pitched under a tree would have water dripping on it for hours after the rain had stopped. The best place to pitch

a tipi was northeast of the trees where it would be shaded from late morning until late afternoon.

A good camp site was as level as possible. It was also important to select a site that was higher than the surrounding area, one that would drain well in wet weather and be safe from floods.

Most bands had a winter camp site that they would return to each fall. They'd begin traveling again early in the spring. But in the course of their journeys, they frequently returned to favorite camp sites along the way and avoided sites that seemed unlucky or held unhappy memories.

Within a camp site, some spots were considered better than others. Women would hurry to pitch their tipis in the most desirable locations.

## Pitching the Tipi

Two women usually worked together to set up a lodge. The cover was spread out on the ground wrong side up. The foundation poles were carefully positioned on top of it. Two poles were placed together, and the third was placed on top of them to make a cross. In this way they marked the place where the poles should be tied at the top of the tipi.

For a three-pole structure they would select their three sturdiest poles because this tripod would form the foundation of the tipi. One woman would take a long rope and tie the three poles together at the cross. Then the women would raise the tripod.

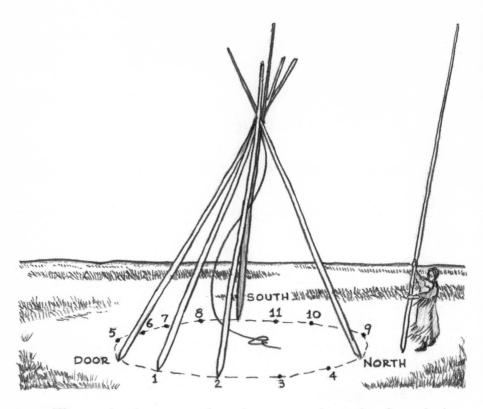

The pole that was placed on top when the foundation poles were positioned on the cover was the door pole and was located just to the left of the doorway as you entered the tipi. Since Indian tipis usually faced east, the door pole was positioned on the east side when the tripod was raised. The other poles were put toward the back of the tipi at the north and south.

The three poles locked into place to form a strong foundation for the tipi. The order and placement of each pole in the frame was important. The first four poles of the frame were put in position from the doorway moving

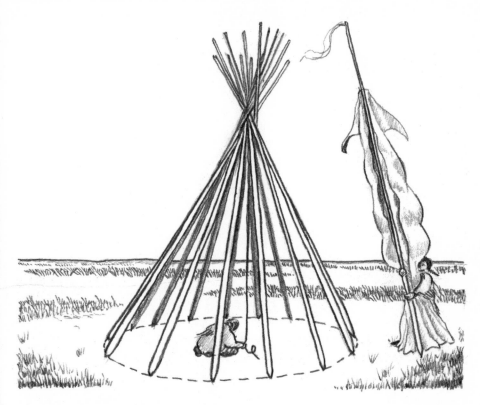

toward the north. The tops of these poles all rested in the front crotch of the tripod, the V shape formed at the top, front of the foundation poles. The next four frame poles were put in place from the door pole to the south tripod pole. They rested on top of the first four frame poles in the same crotch, putting most of the poles—two-thirds of them—in the same fork of the foundation. This created the least possible bulk under the cover and kept the place where the poles crossed as trim as possible.

Poles 9, 10, and 11 were positioned in the back be-

35

tween the north and south tripod poles, leaving a space between pole 10 and pole 11 for the last frame pole. These poles all rested in the rear forks of the foundation poles.

Then the women took the long rope that was used to tie the tripod and wrapped it around all the poles that were now standing. They went around four times and the rope was then tied to an anchor peg inside the tipi, near the center. In times of heavy winds, this made the structure more secure.

The last frame pole was called the lifting pole. It was

used to lift the cover onto the frame. The women positioned the lifting pole on the cover, tied the cover to the pole, and folded it into a bundle. Then they hoisted the lifting pole into its place at the back of the tipi between poles 10 and 11.

The women would bring the cover around the poles on opposite sides and meet at the door pole. The left side of the cover was crossed over the right side and the cover held together with lacing pins. Lacing pins were pointed sticks about the size of pencils. They were made from chokecherry, ash, or dogwood. The women had to climb up on something to reach high enough to insert the lacing pins at the top. Lacing pins were inserted from right to left. A line of eleven or more pins extended down the front of the cover to fasten it securely.

Next the women went inside the tipi and adjusted all the poles by pushing them out against the cover as far as they would go. If the Indians planned to camp there for a while, or if the area was swept by high winds, they would make holes and sink the pole butts several inches into the ground. This kept the poles from slipping. Finally, the smoke-flap poles were put in place and the smoke flaps stretched tight.

The cover of the tipi was firmly anchored by wooden pegs placed at regular intervals around the base of the cover. Some twenty-five chokecherry or ash pegs were used. Each peg was about 2 feet long and an inch thick. They were sharpened to a point at one end. Some of the bark was left on at the other end to prevent the cover

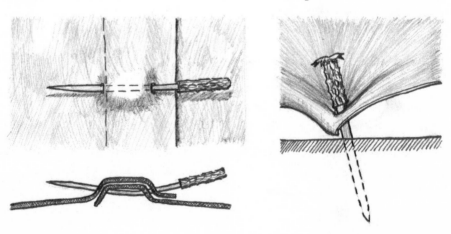

from sliding up the peg. The pegs were driven into the ground through holes or loops at the bottom of the cover.

A stake or forked branch was set in front of the tipi. Long cords attached to the bottom of the smoke flaps were tied to the stake. This helped to keep the smoke flaps taut and was an additional brace to secure the tipi.

If the Indians were going to be in camp for a long time or if heavy rains seemed likely, they dug a narrow ditch around the base of the tipi with a run-off at the lowest place so that water would drain away from the tipi.

## Tribal Differences Among Tipis

Some tribes used a four-pole foundation. A four-pole foundation forms a rectangular base. The front and back (east and west) sides would be the short sides of the rectangle. The two long sides would be on the north and south.

The Blackfoot, Comanche, and Crow were some of the people who used a four-pole foundation. The Dakota or Sioux, Cheyenne, Kiowa, Arapaho, and Assiniboin were three-pole people.

The lodge poles of some tribes extended high above the tops of the lodge, giving the tipi the appearance of an hourglass. Some tribes used shorter lodge poles,

which gave their lodges a cut-off appearance. Three-pole tipis usually had pockets in which to insert the smoke-flap poles, while four-pole tipis usually had holes in the tips of the smoke flaps through which the poles passed. Sometimes the back of the tipi was almost straight up and down while the front had a long gentle slope. Four-pole tipis tended to be less tilted than three-pole ones. The smoke-flap poles of some tipis crossed at the back when the smoke flaps were wide open. In other tipis the smoke-flap poles just met at the back. The smoke flaps of four-pole tipis were generally set farther apart. The smoke hole was larger at the top and lower around the poles.

Differences in tipis from tribe to tribe may seem minor, but Indians approaching a strange camp could quickly tell whether they were approaching friends or enemies just by the look of their tipis.

## Camp Circles

Each tipi had its own place within the camp circle. The camp circle was usually a large ring with an opening about 20 yards long on its east side. The lodges were arranged in a specific order—family by family and band by band. The doorway of each tipi in the circle faced east.

Inside the main circle, there was a smaller circle formed by the chief's lodge, council lodge, painted medicine tipis, and the lodges of any special organizations, warrior societies, or dancing fraternities.

Some tribes had camp circles made up of rings of tipis arranged in a large circle. Each small circle represented a band or subdivision of the tribe.

On some important occasions like the Sun Dance, the lodges might face the ceremonial lodge in the center of the circle rather than face east. All the tipis could then draw power from the ceremonial lodge. The Sun Dance was held in the summer, when fires were not necessary to heat the lodges and concerns about wind direction were not great.

In the winter the Indians rarely camped in a circle. They camped instead at a sheltered site along a valley

or river bottom. Then they would pitch their tipis in a line that might extend for miles.

Although Indians kept moving from place to place to follow the buffalo, they moved within the boundaries of their own tribal area. They generally had regular patterns of movement and often returned to the same camp sites. The camp circle was so well organized and the patterns and movements of the tribe so well known by tribal members that hunting parties or war parties could stay away for months and still know where to go to find their people again and where within the camp circle to find their own tipi.

## The Spiritual Importance of Tipis

Indians were deeply religious people, but they did not build churches. Each Indian used his tipi as a place of worship as well as a home. In his tipi, an Indian felt a

close bond with the Great Mystery. Each lodge was a circle within the camp circle, a reminder of the sacred life circle that has no beginning and no end. The tipi held many special reminders of spiritual thoughts for the Indian. The floor represented the earth, the walls represented the sky, and the poles were paths reaching up to the spirit world.

Indians prepared a square of earth behind the fireplace as an altar. Choice pieces of food were sometimes placed on the altar as an offering to the spirits. Incense was burned on it—sweet grass, cedar, or sage—to carry prayers to the Ones Above.

A feast was often held to dedicate a new lodge and to honor the women who made it. Prayers were offered for the long life, success, and happiness of those living in the tipi. The Indians prayed that the lodge would shelter them from storms and protect them from harm.

## Good Tipi Manners

All the families in the camp circle lived close together, so rules for polite behavior were important. By observing these rules, Indians showed respect for each other's feelings and privacy.

If the tipi door was open, all were welcome to come in. If the door flap was closed, a visitor was expected to cough or call out and wait to be invited in. Some tipis had a rattle hung above the entrance which could be used as a doorbell. If the door was tied down and two sticks crossed over the entrance, the door was "locked." Everyone knew that the people who lived there had gone out or did not want to be disturbed.

When entering a tipi, men turned to the right and sat in their places on the north side of the tipi. Women turned to the left and sat on the south side. It was not polite to come between another person and the fire. It was good manners to walk behind others whenever possible.

Visiting, feasting, and good conversation were greatly enjoyed by the Indians. A gathering usually opened with a prayer. Visitors brought their own dishes and eating utensils. A polite host urged his guests to eat as much as they wanted and to take home whatever food was left. Men were served first, and then women and children. The host was always the last to take food.

Good stories and jokes were a welcome part of any Indian gathering. People talked one at a time. No one interrupted the person who was speaking.

When a host wished to signal the end of the gathering, he cleaned his pipe and placed the ashes in a neat pile on the altar. Then everyone knew the feast was over. They got up and went home.

## Traveling from Camp to Camp

When game, fuel, water, and grass became scarce, a decision was made to move to a new site. The evening before moving day, the camp crier would ride through camp announcing the move to better hunting grounds. The chief's lodge was first to come down. By early morning all the tipis would be down and the caravan under way. A camp could be taken down or put up with amazing speed.

Their tipis and belongings were transported on a travois (pronounced *tra*-VOY). The travois was originally used by Indians during the Dog Days. It was later enlarged and adapted to be pulled by horses, but dogs continued to be used as pack animals to carry some things. A travois was a net platform hung between two poles that formed a V shape. The point of the V was fastened between the animal's shoulders and the poles trailed behind on the ground.

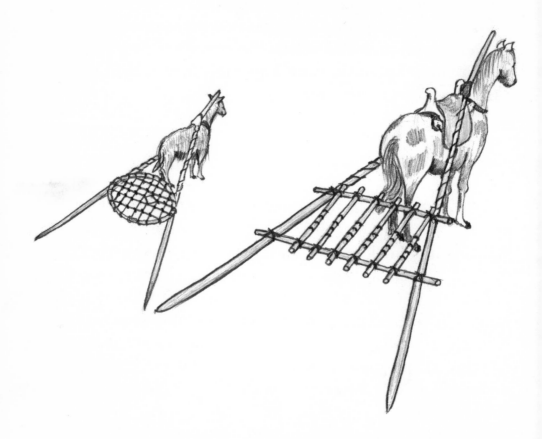

A dog could only haul a bundle weighing between 40 and 80 pounds. Since each lodge pole weighed 15 to 20 pounds and the buffalo-hide cover for a small lodge was over 60 pounds, the horse was very helpful to the Indians when it came time to move camp. A bundle of poles could be hung on each side of the horse with the heavy ends dragging on the ground. One horse could drag eight to ten poles. Three horses could move an average family lodge and all its furnishings. Small children or sick people could be carried on a travois.

Women carried some food and belongings in packs on their backs. Men never carried packs. They needed to keep their arms free so they could use their weapons at any time to fight an enemy or catch game.

A large Indian camp made a grand procession when they were traveling. There were warriors riding in front, boys on ponies, pack horses dragging tipi poles, dogs barking, bells jingling, fringes swinging, and people singing. Soon they would be setting up a new camp on the Great Plains.

# COMFORTS
# AND
# LUXURIES

## CHAPTER FOUR

## *The Lining*

When Indians stopped somewhere overnight, tipis were just pitched as shelters to sleep in. But when they camped in one place for any length of time, they added amenities, things to make the tipi and the camp more pleasant and comfortable to live in.

The lining, or dew cloth, looked like a curtain that went all the way around the inside of the tipi. It was tied to the lodge poles at a height of about six feet and went all the way to the floor.

The lining was an important part of the tipi. It made the lodge a more comfortable place to live. The lining

49

served as insulation, helping to keep the lodge warm in the winter and cool in the summer.

It also improved ventilation, increasing the flow of air in the tipi and preventing the lodge from getting too smoky. As air inside the tipi was warmed by the fire, the warm air would rise and cold air would be drawn in from the outside. The cold air could come in under the cover and go up behind the lining. This flow of air would keep the fire burning well, and smoke from the fire would be drawn out the smoke hole.

The lining kept drafts and dampness away from the living quarters. It kept dew from condensing inside. And it kept any rain dripping off the poles out of the living area. The lining helped keep the lodge dry.

At night the top of the tipi would glow brightly above the lining. Without a lining, the people inside would

cast their shadows on the tipi wall. But there were no shadows when the lining was in place. The lining not only ensured privacy, but it was also important for the safety of the people inside: if an enemy was nearby, shadows would be targets to aim at.

Linings were often decorated with very beautiful designs of beaded stripes, feathers, dyed hair, tassels, or buffalo dewclaws. Men sometimes painted the lining to record experiences. They would illustrate personal triumphs as hunters or warriors or stories about tribal events. The lining added to the beauty of the lodge and made each home a special place. It also added comfort, privacy, and safety to the home.

## Doors

Different kinds of doors were used on tipis. They varied in their shape and decoration. A door might be a hide embellished with designs worked in beads, paint, or quills. Or it might be nothing more than an old blanket attached to the lacing pins above the doorway. (A stick could be fastened across the blanket to stretch it over the door opening).

Some doors were made by stretching a skin between two sticks. Others were stretched on a willow frame that

was bent into an oval or round shape. Some doors were made from buffalo, bear, or other animal skin with the hair left on. Hides with hair left on shed water well and would help keep the entryway dry.

## Furnishings

Indians kept few belongings. They had to be able to pack everything they owned quickly and be able to move easily from camp to camp. But even with limited furnishings, the Indians' homes provided them with some luxury.

Furs were placed on the floors as ground cloths. Beds were pallets made of buffalo hides. These were put on the ground along the sides and back of the lodge.

Women made willow-rod backrests to provide comfortable places to sit. Peeled willow rods about as thick as pencils were strung together with sinew thread to make a mat. The top of the mat was hung from a tripod —three thin poles which were beautifully painted and carved. The mat rested against two of the poles, and the third was used to adjust the angle of the backrest so that

a person could sit up straight or lean back. The lower part of the mat was wider than the top and was laid on the floor to make a seat. In winter a buffalo robe might be hung over the mat for extra warmth. These backrests were usually kept at the head of the bed.

Beautifully decorated rawhide storage boxes or envelopes, called parfleches, were kept behind the beds. These were used to store food, clothing, and personal belongings. When the Indians traveled, they slung their

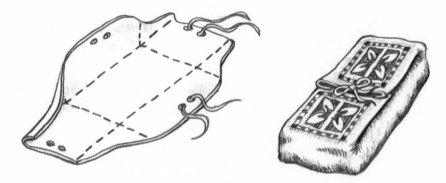

parfleches on either side of the pack saddle, so these were often made in pairs, each pair being decorated exactly alike.

The fireplace was the center of the home, and everything was placed symmetrically around it. Furnishings and belongings were arranged to give a balanced and neat appearance to the tipi. The rear of the lodge, opposite the door, was the place of honor. It was the least drafty spot, and no one had to pass between there and the fire to go anywhere in the tipi. The head of the household or an important guest sat in the place of honor.

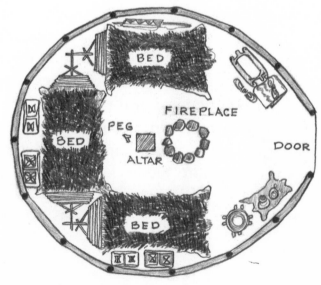

Religious and sacred objects were stored at the back of the lodge. Riding gear was kept north of the door, off to the right as you entered the tipi. Weapons were stored on the north side too. Fuel for the fireplace was kept south of the door, to the left as you entered. All food, household equipment and utensils, and all women's belongings were stored on the south side of the lodge. Water hung from a tipi pole in a bag made from the lining of a buffalo's stomach. The pipe bag, storage pouches, and a variety of other items hung from the poles of the tipi.

## Heating, Cooling, and Lighting

A tipi was cheerful and comfortable all year round. In spring the moon would shine through the smoke hole and cast a silvery light. In winter the snowy plains would seem very still and the morning light that filled the tipi was pale and soft.

For most of the year the fire in the center of the tipi provided all necessary heat and light as well as a place to cook meals. Finding firewood on the treeless prairie was difficult, however. There was some available wood from shrubs and the few trees that did grow on the plains, but a major source of fuel was buffalo chips (dried buffalo dung). These made a hot low flame that produced little smoke.

Large piles of fuel were placed in several locations in the camp. Keeping a good supply of fuel on hand was a community project. All the women, old men, and boys who were able were expected to help gather fuel. Each family could go to the nearest pile when they needed fuel for their tipi. No one went without fuel. Even those who were sick or unable to help gather fuel were provided for.

In a well-selected camp site that provided as much shelter as possible, the central fireplace kept the tipi warm during most of the winter. In extremely cold weather, poles and brush were formed into a windbreak ten to twelve feet high around the tipi.

In the summer the tipi lining provided enough insulation to keep the lodge comfortably cool. In extremely hot weather the cover and the lining were lifted about 3

feet off the ground and propped up on forked sticks. This improved the flow of air in the tipi. If it was very hot but also very windy, branches of trees and shrubs were leaned against the southwest side of the tipi. This kept the sunlight out of the tipi and helped break the heat.

Sometimes a *wicky*, or *squaw cooler*, was put up in hot weather. Four forked poles were placed in the ground to form a rectangle. Poles were laid across the top from fork

to fork. Other poles were laid on top crossing these. Then the top was covered with leafy branches held down by poles placed on top of that. This made an airy outdoor porch.

In hot weather, cooking fires were built outside, but when it was very windy, a kitchen tipi was sometimes set up. This was an old tipi with the bottom cut off. Here the Indians could prepare meals, maintaining a safe, even fire without heating up their homes.

## *A Bath Lodge*

For routine washing the Indians went to a river or stream. Being clean and purified was an important part of their religious life. Plains Indians made a sweat lodge, similar to a steam bath, which could be used by four to six people.

Twelve or fourteen willow shoots about as thick as a man's thumb were set in the ground to form a circle about seven feet across. The door faced east. Opposite willow shoots were bent into arches and twisted together to form a round dome-shaped frame. The frame was completely covered with hides. The floor was covered with sweet sage. The sweat lodge had a pit, into which red-hot stones were placed. When the leader threw water on the hot stones, the lodge would fill with hissing steam. In a sweat lodge, it was possible to get very clean in the coldest weather using little water. But the lodge had ceremonial as well as practical significance, and the procedure was a carefully performed ritual.

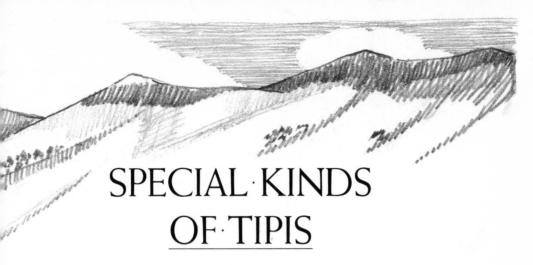

# SPECIAL·KINDS OF·TIPIS

## CHAPTER FIVE

### *The Chief's Tipi*

The chief's tipi, pitched inside the camp circle, was no grander than the other lodges. It could be identified by his emblem—a horse's tail or scalp—fastened to the lifting pole. When the lifting pole was in place, the chief's emblem hung above the entrance to his tipi.

Indians thought of their chief as the father of his people. He was called upon to help members of the tribe who were in need. He was expected to be kind and generous. Since the chief entertained a lot and had frequent visitors and guests in his home, his tipi might be one of the largest in the camp. However, he shared his

61

food and his possessions with the people in his tribe. He kept what he needed for himself and his family, but gave away many of his finest things.

## Council Lodges

The council lodge was also set up inside the camp circle. Here the council would meet to discuss tribal matters and conduct ceremonies. The lodge was rarely furnished, but it was always a very large tipi because it had to hold many people.

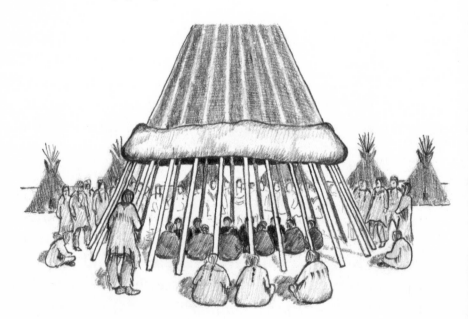

## Tipis for Special Societies

Within the tribe were various groups and organizations that had special functions related to warfare, hunting, and camp discipline. These societies would see that the tribal council's orders were carried out, supervise moving and make sure that each tipi was in its proper place, organize tribal hunts, or serve as camp policemen. Some societies were the keepers of special wisdom or skills. This special knowledge was often revealed in a vision by a spirit. Each society had its own songs and ceremonies and its own lodge pitched in the inner camp circle. These lodges were used for meetings, feasts, dances, and rituals.

## Children's Tipis

Small lodges were sometimes set up as children's playhouses. These might be made from old lodge covers and poles. A little girl could begin learning how to make a tipi by helping make a playhouse or a small lodge for a doll. Children sometimes played with miniature camp circles, using tiny tipis made from leaves and sticks.

## Burial Lodges

Most people were buried in a natural cave or crevice formed among the rocks or placed in a hole just large enough and deep enough for the body. But sometimes when an important person died, his body was left in his lodge. He was dressed in his finest things—painted robes, headdress, feathers, and jewelry—and placed on the bed. The tipi was left fully furnished. The cover was securely fastened all around the bottom, and the smoke flaps were closed. The door was tied shut and blocked with poles and branches. His medicine bundle was tied to the top of the lodge poles. The tipi was left

undisturbed on the plains. If the tribe returned to the place of the burial lodge in the course of its travels, the Indians usually held a second period of mourning.

## Medicine Lodges

A tipi with paintings on the cover was a special medicine lodge. Only a small number of tipis were painted. A medicine lodge was a sacred object, and it was a great honor to own one. These treasured possessions usually belonged to important tribal members—chiefs, leaders of war parties, or medicine men. They were set up inside the main camp circle.

The word *medicine* is a misleading translation of an Indian word. Indians used the word for all that was spiritual, holy, mysterious, or supernatural. A medicine man was not primarily a doctor to the Indians, although at times he was called on to use his powers to try to heal or cure. Men who had medicine in the Indian meaning of the word were holy men. They were prophets, the spiritual leaders of the tribe.

A medicine lodge was usually first owned by an animal spirit. The animal would appear in a dream or vision to an Indian who was worthy and in need of help. The animal spirit promised to give the Indian some of his power. This power would be a painted lodge and other sacred objects. The animal showed the Indian the lodge and gave detailed instructions on making the sacred objects associated with the powers. He instructed the Indian in the songs, ceremonies, and rituals that would be part of his medicine. When the man awoke, he'd carefully follow the directions. The holy objects were kept in medicine bundles, special fringed rawhide cases. Medicine bundles were hung from a tripod behind the tipi during the day and brought inside at night.

When a medicine lodge cover became worn, the same design was copied on the new cover. The owner might invite some people known to be of good character to join him for a smoke. By smoking the pipe, they gave their consent to help with the painting. He might also seek aid from someone who was especially skilled as an artist. The lodge was set up and stretched into shape. The old lodge cover was kept nearby to be measured and copied. Areas of color and outlines of figures or designs were blocked in. Then the cover was spread out on the ground to be completed. Paints were rubbed into the hide. Willow sticks were used for rulers, buffalo tails or porous bones were used for brushes, and cut rawhide circles were used as patterns to outline disks. Paints were obtained from the earth—brown, red, yellow, and white clays. Mud and charcoal were used for black. Green and blue could be produced from copper ores or from clays. Buffalo yellow was made from the buffalo gallstones. Commercial powdered paints were a popular trade item with the Indians. Pigments were stored in skin bags. The powder was mixed with water. Sometimes a gluey substance made of buffalo tendons or beaver tail was mixed into the paint or applied later as a varnish. Prepared paints were put in separate paint pots made from hollow stones or turtle shells.

The owner of the new lodge dedicated it by inviting the owners of other painted lodges in the camp to pray with him there.

An old medicine lodge cover could not be made into clothing as was the practice with ordinary tipis. Instead, it had to be staked out on the ground as an offering to the sun. Or it was spread out on water and weighted down with stones as an offering to the water spirits.

The right to use a medicine tipi design was handed down from generation to generation. Owners were careful to transfer these rights only to a relative by blood or marriage and only to someone worthy of the honor, someone who would uphold the responsibilities of owning such a tipi. Owners feared that misfortune or death would afflict their family if the tipi passed into other hands.

It was possible to buy the rights to a medicine tipi or to be given a painted tipi. But, the proper rituals had to be carefully observed when transferring all the rights and powers. If the owner and his family were enjoying good health and good fortune, they would be reluctant to part with their painted tipi. If things were not going well—if there was a death in the family or bad luck—they would be more willing to sell the rights to the medicine lodge.

On rare occasions, if a relative was in great need of the medicine, the tipi design could be loaned to the relative to make one time. The family could live there until the cover wore out, but they could not renew the design or make any future claim to it. Only the rightful owner could use that design.

It was not necessary to renew the medicine lodge to maintain the right to use it. The owner could make a painted lodge of that design at any time he wished. No other person could copy that design even if the owner was not using it. Some owners lived in their medicine tipis for so many years that they were identified with their tipis, becoming known by names like Red Tipi Man or Black-Striped Tipi Man.

There were often certain restrictions or taboos associated with using medicine lodges. One became known as the sausage picture tipi because eating sausages or intestines was forbidden inside it. The Indians believed that anyone who ate sausages there would get blisters on the lips. The lodge had nineteen horizontal red stripes painted all the way around the cover.

The moon tipi had powerful medicine, but it also had a powerful taboo. Boys were never to play in it. If they did, it was believed that the owner would be shot in battle or would break a bone hunting. The son of the

moon tipi's owner never used his right to the lodge because he feared this taboo. The tipi had a light blue crescent moon in the center of the back and one in the center of the front. Two large dark blue wedges covered each side. The top and the remainder of the front and back were painted red.

Medicine tipis were primarily holy objects. But even though it was only of secondary importance to the Indians, these tipis were also works of art. Each tipi was a mural of beautiful, bold design.

The primary colors—red, yellow and blue—were most frequently used. Green, brown, and black were used more sparingly. Tipis were usually decorated with three colors or less, and rarely was one painted with more than four colors.

Most tipis were designed in four basic formats. Within this limited range of color and layout, the Indians achieved wide variety and originality of design:

(1) Some tipis were painted in one solid color with small areas in a different color. These accents were usually painted at the back of the tipi near the top.

(2) Another commonly used format divided the cover into three bands. The areas at the top and bottom were smaller and painted in a dark color. The middle area was painted a light color or left unpainted. The top band symbolized the sky and the spirit world. It often had unpainted circles representing stars. The bottom band represented earthly things. This, too, might have rows of unpainted circles going around it to represent fallen stars or puffballs. (Puffballs are round white plants that look like mushrooms. They burst when touched, and brown powder puffs out.) Animals, symbolic designs, or scenes were painted in the large middle area. This for-

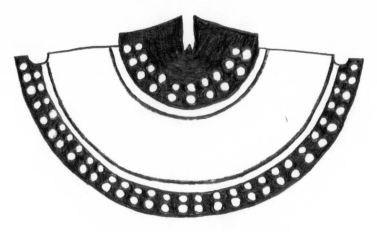

mat was very practical since the two darkly painted areas were the parts of the tipi which quickly became dark with normal use—the top, which was near the smoke hole, and the bottom, which was close to the ground and mud.

(3) Other tipis were covered with horizontal stripes that went all the way around the tipi.

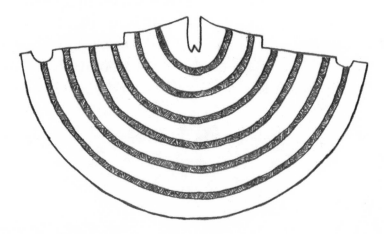

(4) On still other painted lodges, the cover was divided into two halves down the center of the back. Each half could be treated separately. There might be a pic-

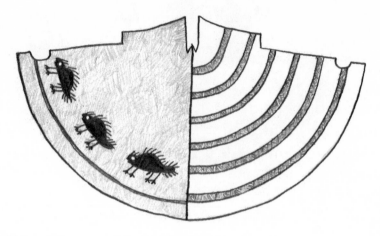

ture of animal spirits on one half and stripes on the other. Or there might be a symmetrical, balanced design using symbolic shapes, animal figures, or a combination of both.

Many symbols were used in the painting of tipis. A painted circle representing the sun often appeared at the top of the tipi's back. A painted crescent represented the moon. Unpainted circles or diamond shapes on a solid background stood for stars. A maltese cross stood

for the morning star and was believed to bring powerful dreams to the lodge owner. A row of triangles or round projections from the bottom band around the tipi represented hills or mountains. Half-ovals were rocks, and the thunderbird symbolized lightning. Straight or arched parallel lines of different colors symbolized the rainbow, the clearing storm. Red, white, and blue bands stood for the red morning cloud or rising sun, the white cloud, and the blue sky. Black represented night.

Indians believed animals had supernatural powers and often pictured them on medicine lodges. The sacred character of the animal was shown by a lifeline leading from the animal's mouth to its heart and kidneys. The lifeline was believed to be the source of these animals' power. Otters, elk, snakes, horses, porcupines, turtles, eagles, and some mythical beasts were represented on medicine lodge covers.

The buffalo and bear were frequently painted. The buffalo was a symbol of generosity, abundance, and hard work. Buffalo had great powers to bestow as well as the power to keep men free from want. Bears also had powerful medicine. They could give courage, wisdom, magic, and knowledge of herbal medicine.

Actual experiences in battle or the hunt were sometimes portrayed, but paintings of visionary and religious experiences were more frequently painted.

Lone Chief of the Kiowa-Apache tribe had a vision. He saw a huge bear grasping a tipi with his four legs wrapped all the way around it. The bear told Lone Chief that if he made this tipi, the bear spirit would always protect him and hold him up.

The bear tipi that Lone Chief painted had a huge blue bear on a solid red background. The bear had a long, thin body extending up the center of the back of the tipi. It had a small head at the top of the tipi and a stubby tail pointing to the ground. The bear's legs were very long and very thin. They encircled and seemed to grasp the tipi. A small blue crescent moon was painted above the bear's head, and there was a small blue sun above the moon. The door was a bear hide with the fur removed from the center and a border of fur left around the edge.

This tipi was considered good and powerful medicine. When the tipi was made and the proper prayers said, it was believed that the bear would cure a sick family member. There was a widespread belief among Indians in the bear's power to cure illness. Indians said that they acquired their knowledge of herbal medicine by follow-

ing bears and studying the plants bears ate.

It was considered taboo for anyone except a member of the hereditary family to sleep in the bear tipi. And when it wore out, the old tipi cover was to be carefully staked on the plains with the bear's head facing the rising sun.

Lone Chief passed the rights to this tipi on to his son. His son gave him his best horse for the tipi. When the son died, the rights passed to his sister. She passed them on to her son, White Man. White Man was among the chiefs who negotiated in Washington on behalf of their people. He died around 1900. Neither White Man nor his mother ever renewed the tipi. The bear tipi was last made around 1865.

# WHAT·HAPPENED TO·TIPIS

## AFTERWORD

As the settlers pushed westward, there was a constant struggle to take over the land. In about five years, unrestrained buffalo hunting wiped out the huge herds of buffalo that had once covered the Great Plains. A buffalo would be killed for a small part—the tongue or horns—and the rest left to rot on the prairie. By 1883 the buffalo were gone. The source of the Indians' food, clothing, and shelter was destroyed. Their way of life was destroyed. Previously unknown diseases, such as smallpox, wiped out entire tribes. Indians were confined to reservations. They were issued food rations. Their children were sent to boarding schools to be taught English and the ways of the white man. In many places tipis were prohibited by law. Indians were issued drafty, cheerless, uncomfortable housing that had no medicine.

Many Indians are trying to keep their culture and traditions alive. Camp circles are still being formed for special ceremonies and events, and tipis stand as majestic reminders of the Buffalo Days.

# INDEX

DAVID YUE was born in Shanghai, China, and moved to the United States at an early age. He graduated from the University of Pennsylvania with a Master of Architecture degree. CHARLOTTE YUE was born in Philadelphia and also graduated from the University of Pennsylvania. They live in Philadelphia with their children, Frances and Timothy. *The Tipi* is their first book for Knopf.